CHRIST IN THE WORKPLACE:
An Employee Handbook

Printed in the United States of America

Publisher: We Family Ministries
P.O. Box 40644
Jacksonville, FL 32203

Library of Congress Cataloging pending
ISBN: 0-9788545-5-1

WELCOME

Welcome

Welcome to the body of Christ where you have the opportunity to impact the lives of all who come in contact with you for the glory of God. This position requires commitment to the things of God at all times.

This booklet was written to give you answers to those most often asked questions about "human" resource policies, procedures, and benefits. It explains what God expects from you and what you can expect to receive from him for your obedience. It also describes the power of your combined efforts with the Father to enrich not only your life but the lives of all those who come in contact with you.

The growth of any organization can he attributed to the knowledge, skill, and commitment of each employee. The more you learn about your employer, Jesus, the better employee you will be. So study this handbook, refer to it often, and if your questions are not answered, talk to the Father.

Serving God wholeheartedly in your workplace makes you an employee with value, strength, and endurance. These attributes enrich your life and allow you to be a blessing to your employer and your fellow employees. God is pleased that you have decided to join his team and honor him by remaining dedicated to his plan and purpose for your life, even in the workplace. For this you will be eternally blessed.

Purpose

This employee handbook has been prepared to give you specific guidelines, policies, and procedures under which you must operate if you want to walk a path that is pleasing to God in the workplace. You will learn how to face workplace challenges by being Christ-like even in the face of overwhelming circumstances. You will understand your authority in Jesus Christ and the victory that comes with welcoming Jesus into your workplace. Although the information in this book has been specifically tailored for the workplace, it can be applied to any area of your life.

This handbook represents a contract, expressed and implied, guaranteeing joy, peace, prosperity, and eternal life. This at-will relationship remains in effect, withstanding all statements to the contrary, as set forth in God's word, the Holy Bible.

Mission Statement

Live an example that will claim disciples in all the nations and teach others to obey everything that God has commanded you to do. Strive for an excellence in service that glorifies Him.

Vision

Live His way in every circumstance and reject anything that is contrary to plan and purpose for your life. His vision is that you be free from what ever binds you including stress, strife, frustration, and indifference.

GENERAL EMPLOYMENT

DAY 1

Equal Employment Policy

The Employer is an equal opportunity employer. It is his policy to enlist and promote individuals as well as oversee all decisions, conditions, and personal actions without regard to race, color, age, religion, sex, national origin, ancestry, marital status, disability, or status of worldly qualifications. In this regard, he will take action as necessary to ensure the safety and well-being of his employees. Any situation believed to be unjust should be brought to his immediate attention for a quick resolution.

Equal Employment

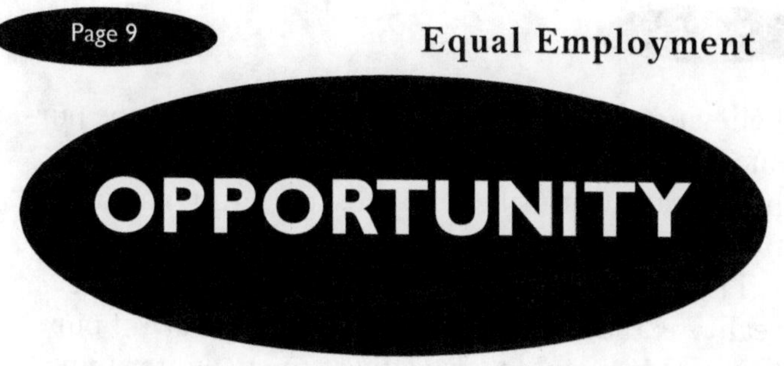

7 But the Lord said to me, "Do not say, 'I am only a child.' You must go to everyone I send you to and say whatever I command you. 8 Do not be afraid of them, for I am with you and will rescue you," declares the Lord. *Jeremiah 1:7-8*

God has called every one of us to four purposes; to worship, to fellowship, to grow, and to serve. He has equipped us with the power through Jesus Christ to perform these tasks. Occasionally, life deals us circumstances that make us feel that we are less than prepared to face these sometimes challenging ordeals. This is especially true in workplaces ruled by pride and arrogance. Our fleshly response is often to respond in timidity or to avoid the situation all together.

It is through Satan's deception that workplace abuse is able to negatively affect our self-worth. Unfortunately lying co-workers, back-stabbing bosses, and disloyal companies can sometimes have that affect on us. As the world's values collide with ours, we become disillusioned by the lie that Christ belongs everywhere in our lives except at work. We are left feeling alone, abandoned, and unequipped for the tasks at hand. Many Christians are deceived by believing that religion is a private matter to be pursued publicly only in the church. Still, many employers foster this belief by discouraging any display of Christianity in the workplace.

This is contradictory to God's will for us. The reality is that Christ reigns over every part of our lives. Why wouldn't we expect to encounter him in the workplace? He is there, working with us to improve the quality of our work and our lives. He knows that our success here on earth demands on his presence to guide us along the path that he has set before us. Christ ensures that all of our works are positive and valuable.

His entire ministry was dedicated to helping others to realize and experience their potential through Christ. He is able to empathize with us because he was one of us. Through his earthly path we were reconciled to God and to one another. Therefore, we have wholeness of body, mind, and spirit. We have eternal life. We are everything God says we are; wonderfully made in Christ's image. Even more important is that these Godly attributes not only make us valuable here on earth but in heaven as well.

When we reject any ideas that separate God and us, we gain security through Him. We recognize that we are righteous because He was righteous. Nothing on earth can take away our place in the kingdom and the freedom, originality, and joy that it brings. We can do all things through Christ who is in our workplace strengthening us every step of the way.

OPPORTUNITY

Lord, as the enemy bombards me with negativity, I proclaim these situations as opportunities to reveal your greatness in me. Thank you that your presence in my workplace has given me victory.

NOTES

DAY 2

Christians with Disabilities

Each employee is expected to make an eternal effort to overcome their disabilities by repentance and the remission of sins. The Employer will provide supernatural accommodations, unconditional love, and undeserved forgiveness, for those with disabilities. He is committed to your healing and restoration.

TEMPTATION

1Therefore, since we are surrounded by such a great cloud of witnesses, let us throw off everything that hinders and the sin that so easily entangles, and let us run with perseverance the race marked out for us. 2Let us fix our eyes on Jesus, the author and perfecter of our faith, who for the joy set before him endured the cross, scorning its shame, and sat down at the right hand of the throne of God. 3Consider him who endured such opposition from sinful men, so that you will not grow weary and lose heart.
Hebrews 12:1-3

In the workplace, we will be faced with many situations where our values clash with the values of the world. We may be faced with a negative or angry co-worker who knows how to push all the right buttons. What about being confronted with gossip or lies about a fellow co-worker or worse, about us. How many times have we been blamed for something we didn't do? For the Christian working in a secular job, the temptations to sin may be overpowering.

No matter what situations we face, we always have a choice in how we react. At times, the temptation to respond as the world would; in anger, frustration, revenge, or defeat seems overwhelming. In times like these, we must overcome by the blood of the lamb and the word of our testimony. (Revelations 12:11)

This precious blood represents an eternal covenant that keeps us holy even in the midst of workplace darkness. Grace and peace covers us and allows us to interact with others while remaining dedicated to the things of God. Our testimony is that treasured blood of Jesus in action. Responding to negativity with concern, patience, and love shows others the Christ in us. This rebukes sin. Our words and actions become a blessing, our weaknesses become strengths, and our disabilities become abilities for God's glory.

Our ability to walk as a Christian is dependent on whether Christ's spirit resides within us. Our own strengths and efforts have no bearing on our ability to resist temptation. To the contrary, our self-sufficiency leads to failure and destruction. Victory over temptation is dependent on our willingness to stay close to God. This willing spirit sustains us. It focuses our attention on Christ. It orders our steps down the path of righteousness. It rebukes sin and the temptation that precedes it. Christ's spirit in us strengthens our confidence in his power and faithfulness. It gives us the courage to step out in faith and give us the opportunity to prove our love for Christ through obedience.

Lord, I know that sin weakens me as a Christian and hinders my walk with you. Thank you for sending your son as a sin offering so that my disabilities become abilities and I can walk upright. Thank you for allowing your righteousness to be fulfilled in me.

NOTES

____

____

____

____

____

____

TEMPTATION

DAY 3

Harassment Policy

Harassment will not be tolerated as it is contradictory to the vision of the Employer. Any employee who believes that he or she is being harassed should immediately notify the Employer who will work for an immediate resolution. All petitions are confidential.

STRESS

5Let your gentleness be evident to all. The Lord is near.
6Do not be anxious about anything, but in everything, by prayer and petition, with thanksgiving, present your requests to God.
7And the peace of God, which transcends all understanding, will guard your hearts and your minds in Christ Jesus. Philippians 4:5-7

Stress in the workplace is a destructive reality for most of us who work a secular job. Unfortunately, it can even be found in some Christian workplaces as well. Many mental health professionals will tell you that the first step to dealing with any problem is to recognize that there is a problem. So first, let us look at stress for exactly what it is. Stress is SIN! It violates God's law and says to the Heavenly Father that we do not have the faith to believe that He is with us, working on our behalf. Stress causes us to grow weary and opens the door for physical, mental, and spiritual illness. It spoils our fruit and hinders our ability to give 100% to God and to our workplace.

Jesus wants to break the bonds of workplace stress. He has given us two main principles by which we can claim victory. Honesty and order are the keys to "Good News" for stress relief.

A great source of workplace stress is the inability to complete tasks for which we have obligated ourselves to. To our employer, this translates to inefficiency, dishonesty, and
in some workplaces, lost revenue. The solution lies in Matthew 5:37. We are commanded to "let our 'Yes' be 'Yes' and our 'No,' be 'No'. Simply put, God wants us to be honest about our abilities and our limitations. Honesty humbles us and reveals that we are powerless without Christ. Yet through him, we can do all things. This belief closes the door to failure and the many pressures it brings.

Stress can also originate from disorder in the workplace. We serve a God of order who commands that we maintain order in every aspect of our life, even the workplace. (1 Corinthians 14:32) Doing so produces peace. For employers this peace in the midst of a stressful situation is interpreted as competence, efficiency, and effectiveness; all desired and valuable assets in the secular workplace. By meeting the needs of our employer for a competent and resourceful workforce, we decrease the opportunities for Satan to torment us with workplace stress.

Stress relief is honoring God through our work and trusting and following his instructions for our lives. Doing so won't completely eliminate stressful situations in the workplace. It will however, help us to succeed in moving our workplace toward morality and order. By working toward God's vision of excellence we gain victory over <u>all</u> of life's challenges. Guaranteed victory is all the stress-relief most of us need.

Lord, it seems that the walls of my workplace demands are closing in on me. Yet, I am reminded that you will not give me more than I can bear. Thank you for your order that allows me to accomplish the tasks at hand and your peace that sustains me while I do.

NOTES

____

____

____

____

____

____

ABOUT YOUR JOB

DAY 4

Identification Badges

All employees are required to wear the identification badge at all times. It should be displayed in plain view. If your identification badge is lost or stolen, you must pay for a replacement. The cost is confession, repentance, and the return to righteousness.

34"A new command I give you: Love one another. As I have loved you, so you must love one another. 35By this all men will know that you are my disciples, if you love one another." John 13:34-35

We live in a universe governed by God, who is love. Love is the principle behind everything we are and everything we do. We are created to love and it demonstrates our faith even beyond our actions. As we practice Christ's values of love in our workplace, he will stand with us and share his power and authority with us.

Conflict in the workplace is always around us. Unfortunately, it may never go away. Most of us are fully aware of its presence and its potential to cause harm. If we allow its destruction to dictate our outcomes then it has the potential to cause serious damage to our relationship with God, our co-workers, and even our families.

Love covers a multitude of sin. It cast out the fear and doubt that often leads to conflict. It breaks the hold of the selfishness that is the catalyst for a significant amount of workplace conflict. Love makes us quick to listen, slow to speak, and slow to anger. It helps us to understand the needs of others as a priority to our own. Love speaks the truth at all times. Love is honesty, loyalty, and faith. Love is faith in action. Love believes that Christ is in control of every situation and that justice always prevails.

When faced with discord in the workplace, many of us are caught off guard. We forget that Christ is in the workplace, not only watching our reaction but tempering our actions with love. We must learn from Jesus and apply his methods of love and patience during controversy. Doing so will equip us with the tools necessary to persevere in the face of adversity, grow in the face of impediments, and claim victory where defeat seems sure.

Lord, I know that your desire is that I bear good fruit. Thank you for your example of love that helps me to walk in obedience and to love others as you have loved me.

DAY 5

Employee Categories

Types of Employees

Probationary (wayside)

When anyone hears the message about the kingdom and does not understand it, the evil one comes and snatches away what was sown in his heart. This is the seed sown along the path.

Temporary (rocky ground)

The one who received the seed that fell on rocky places is the man who hears the word and at once receives it with joy. But since he has no root, he lasts only a short. time.
When trouble or persecution comes because of the word, he quickly falls away.

Part-time (thorny)

The one who received the seed that fell among the thorns is the man who hears the word, but the worries of this life and the deceitfulness of wealth choke it, making it unfruitful.

Full-time (good soil)

The one who received the seed that fell on good soil is the man who hears the word and understands it. He produces a crop, yielding a hundred, sixty or thirty times what was sown.

SEARCH

3Then he told them many things in parables, saying: "A farmer went out to sow his seed. 4As he was scattering the seed, some fell along the path, and the birds came and ate it up. 5Some fell on rocky places, where it did not have much soil. It sprang up quickly, because the soil was shallow. 6But when the sun came up, the plants were scorched, and they withered because they had no root. 7Other seed fell among thorns, which grew up and choked the plants. 8Still other seed fell on good soil, where it produced a crop—a hundred, sixty or thirty times what was sown. 9He who has ears, let him hear." Matthew 13:3-9

Like God, Satan is also an equal opportunity employer. He sends workplace trials and the wounds they cause to distract and deter us from God's purpose for our life. Satan seeks to trick us into believing that we have been abandoned to face life's challenges alone. So it is said, the great deceiver comes to deceive us. Surprise, surprise, surprise!

We as believers must be prepared to do battle 24 hours a day, 7 days a week, 365 days a year. Satan does not take a day off and neither should we. Doing battle means sowing God's word into our hearts and refusing under any circumstance to stray away from it. We must dig our feet in and stand on God's reality, not that of the world. Rely on Jesus' power to accomplish all things according to his will. He will keep us safe and strong.

Producing a 100-fold crop in the workplace requires that

we walk closely with God every single day. Surrender to his lordship and allow his voice to order our steps. As we do, we grow in confidence, hope, and strength. As we increase our understanding of his truths we gain the wisdom and discernment necessary for spiritual success and earthly advancement. Being able to see with the eyes of God's heart makes us a living witness to the truths that will free us, our workplace, and its employees from dysfunction and destruction. Productivity in the workplace requires that we be obedient and committed seed planted and rooted in the good soil of God's word.

Lord. I want to be a seed that is planted on good soil. Thank you for giving me an understanding of your word so that I can apply it to my life and produce a 100-fold crop for your glory.

EMPLOYEE CATEGORIES

DAY 6

Trial Period

All employees are to expect that trials will come. Employees are expected to face these trials with pure joy. The Employer guarantees that these trials will be temporary and that through them employees will gain perseverance, maturity, and completeness.

*2Consider it pure joy, my brothers, whenever you face
trials of many kinds, 3because you know that the testing of
your faith develops perseverance. 4Perseverance must
finish its work so that you may be mature and complete,
not lacking anything. 5If any of you lacks wisdom, he
should ask God, who gives generously to all without
finding fault, and it will be given to him. 6But when he
asks, he must believe and not doubt, because he who doubts
is like a wave of the sea, blown and tossed by the wind.
7That man should not think he will receive anything from
the Lord; 8he is a double-minded man, unstable in all he
does. 1 James 2-8*

In today's workplace where our worth is determined by our compliance not our completeness, conflict is bound to happen. For many, these situations are difficult if not overwhelming. But getting to know Jesus as a man who faced conflict daily yet overcame will help you to gain the vision for victory. The life and ministry of Jesus is the perfect conflict resolution manual. He faced conflict throughout his entire life yet even in death, he overcame.

Jesus' example of conflict resolution encompasses two main principles, love and wisdom.

Whenever Jesus faced objectionable people, he always countered their attacks with love. Even during his occasional angry rebukes, he tempered his own actions with love. When we face conflict in the workplace, we too must apply love as patience, concern, and respect for the other person's wellbeing. We must be willing to commit to remaining righteous not just being right.

Wisdom allows us to see that as we love our opponents, we live out God's will for our lives. This is truly why God created us. Wisdom tells us that if we choose not to love our opponent through the conflict or they choose not to reciprocate our love, then this is clearly sin. There will be consequences for that sin. God is the God of justice. Wisdom reminds us to make room for God to move in our lives through humility and faith. He will mediate the situation for his glory.

So, when people in the workplace stab us in the back, tell lies on us, or do any of the hundreds of things people do to harm others, we have a choice. We can choose the easy road of survival and revenge or the sometimes tenuous road of love and patience. Survival by revenge may give us immediate relief but consider the long-term effects. It jeopardizes our existence in eternity. On the other hand, love may result in us losing the occasional battle, but with love Jesus overcame and so will we.

DOUBT

Lord, though I am faced with trials and tribulations, I will not give in. Thank you for your faithfulness in giving me victory over sin and for helping me to persevere. Thank you for making me mature and complete so that my love for you supersedes my fear and doubt.

NOTES

DAY 7

Wage Determination

Each employee will be paid wages according to his or her deeds. Merit increases and overtime pay is commensurate with your job responsibilities. The Employer reserves the right to garnish your wages for substandard work performance (sin). Prolonged substandard performance will result in "death".

COMPLAINING

22But now that you have been set free from sin and have become slaves to God, the benefit you reap leads to holiness, and the result is eternal life. 23For the wages of sin is death, but the gift of God is eternal life in Christ Jesus our Lord. Romans 6:22-23

So much of what we waste our time and energy on in the workplace will not matter, even an hour from now, much less for eternity. As we spend our time complaining about our work space, job functions, company expectations, we lose focus of what is important. This is why it is so important to shift our prospective from a "here and now" thinking to eternal thinking. We must distinguish the important from the insignificant, the seen from the unseen.

The seen is our current workplace in its current state with all of its current problems. The unseen is all of the wonderful things that God has in store for us. It is all of the amazing blessings promised in his word. The unseen is peace, joy, and prosperity. It is order, justice, and efficiency. It is success in every work.

Worldly promotion and earthly accomplishments are insignificant when compared to their cost to our peace and tranquility. What's important is our intimate relationship with Christ, even at work. It is our family, friends, and even our enemies. Our family and friends contribute greatly to our quality of life. Surrounding ourselves with people who support us when we are up, comfort us when we are down, and correct us when we are wrong; contributes positively to our lives. In the presence of optimism and hope, the temptation to complain is destroyed. Avoiding the temptation to complain also requires that we realize the importance of our adversaries to our spiritual growth. As we see them as opportunities to lay up spiritual treasures and eternal deposits we are discouraged from the temptation to sin in the hope of pleasing God and reaping an eternal reward.

God's mission will be accomplished and we have a responsibility to fulfill our role within His plan. We do this by fixing our eyes on the bigger picture and looking past our current circumstances to the vision that God has for us and our life. This encompasses everything that is important to God; love, patience, joy, and effectiveness. It rejects those things that he rejects; anger, frustration, insecurity, and disappointment. We must store up treasures in heaven by investing our time, talents, and treasures in people for his glory. Doing so will not only allow us to live a fruitful life here on earth. We also make an investment in eternity.

Lord, I know that the wages of sin is death. I want to live. Thank you for helping me to sow righteousness so that I may reap a sure reward.

NOTES

____

____

____

____

____

____

DAY 8

Contributions

The Employer will provide all employees with irrevocable gifts. All gifts must be used to build up the workplace for His glory.

1As he looked up, Jesus saw the rich putting their gifts into
the temple treasury. 2He also saw a poor widow put in two
very small copper coins. 3"I tell you the truth," he said, "this
poor widow has put in more than all the others. 4All these
people gave their gifts out of their wealth; but she out of her
poverty put in all she had to live on." Luke 21:1-4

Utilizing our gifts in the workplace demands that we cast aside any negative thoughts about ourselves. We are made in the image of God, whose very nature is to work. His work is creating and giving meaning to everything on earth, even us. We are the result of God's will, his creativity, and his work. His will is that we fulfill his sacred and meaningful purpose for our lives through the utilization of our God-given gifts.

We are creative beings. We have been blessed with gifts and talents that are given to us to be used for God's glory. God inspires us to recognize our creativity and to do something positive with it. As we perform these works, with God, everything we do is good. He provides us with unlimited resources to ensure that through our gifts his creations prosper. Using our gifts for good, celebrates our intimacy with God and the many treasures hidden within our acts of obedience and our displays of love and compassion.

With God, we have created an endless number of things from music to medicine. If your gift is singing, sing unto the Lord. Maybe you are a writer; write stories that tell of the awesome God we serve. Maybe you are good with numbers, help others to steward their blessings. No matter what God has anointed you to do, you are blessed to be a blessing. Use your gifts for his glory, in the workplace and in life.

Lord, whether my gifts be prophesying, serving, teaching, encouraging, or contributing; let me use them with mercy, diligence, and joy. Thank you for your grace through which I have these gifts and your mercy that proclaims me worthy to use them.

DAY 9

Meetings

All employees must participate in regular meetings with the Employer. These are necessary to keep you on the path that he has set before you. These meetings allow time for you to humbly present questions and concerns. They also allow you and the Employer to discuss matters that enrich your life.

6Do not be anxious about anything, but in everything, by prayer and petition, with thanksgiving, present your requests to God. 7And the peace of God, which transcends all understanding, will guard your hearts and your minds in Christ Jesus. Philippians 4:6-7

In the workplace, the daily challenges of dealing with customers, other employees, the employer, and governmental agencies can be endless. Working with those who climb the backs of other employees to the top of the corporate ladder or those who are dysfunctional, dismissive, manipulative, or just plan mean can take its toll on us. As upsetting as these behaviors is the fact that unfortunately, they may never change. Serving God definitely does not give you immunity to these struggles. The temporary relief of job-hopping or complaining to other employees may sound tempting. These caustic behaviors are not answer. Jesus Christ is the only long-term solution.

In Philippians 4, Paul gives us two very important details about overcoming trials. He stresses the power of prayer and thanksgiving to help claim victory over workplace worries. We must rejoice in all things knowing that Jesus hears our prayers and is always willing to help us. This keeps our focus on what is positive, meaningful, and life-enriching. God rewards this faithful commitment and gratefulness by replacing our anxieties with peace. We must live in a place of thankfulness not only for what we have but for what is to come. This keeps us from focusing on the workplace as it is but seeing it the way God sees it; productive, effective, and fruitful.

As negativity intrudes our lives we must avoid dwelling on it. We cannot allow pessimism to discourage and deflect our attention from God. We must focus on the positives and allow God to reward our obedience with divine peace, even in the midst of our storm. We must trust that the God of justice we serve is faithful to fulfill all of his promises. These promises guarantee a peace that surpasses all understanding, a timely resolution to all of life's challenges, and success in every good work.

Lord, I want to focus on what is true, noble, right, pure, trustworthy, and admirable. Thank you for welcoming me into your presence where I gain clear direction for my life through your quiet and gentle instructions. Thank you for the peace that my obedience brings.

DAY 10

Personnel Records

Personnel records will be kept on all employees and comprise every aspect of the employee's work performance. You can gain unlimited access to your record by submitting a verbal request to the Employer for insight and wisdom. All requests are confidential.

21Then Peter came to Jesus and asked, "Lord, how many times shall I forgive my brother when he sins against me? Up to seven times?" 22Jesus answered, "I tell you, not seven times, but seventy-seven times. Matthew 18:21-22

In the workplace, our commitment to Godly values can make us feel like an outsider. Honesty, humility, and loyalty are often seen as weaknesses in the secular workplace. In some instances they become motives for maltreatment, disregard, or punishment. This abuse may at times sadden us. Other times we may feel angered by the cruelty and neglect. We can find solace in an ever-present God who constantly reminds us that our actions are not in vain.

In our pain we must turn to God. Let him teach us how to forgive; forgive ourselves and others. This has not only earthly value in helping us to experience joy in the workplace but it has eternal value by rebuking the feelings of anger, frustration, and disappointment that can accompany carrying a grudge or trying to get even. Carrying a grudge only hurts the person carrying the grudge. It is self-inflicted pain in disguise. Many times the person or people with whom we have the grudge, do not even notice. For them, life goes on. For us, life becomes hindered and joy hampered.

Matthew 18 tells the story of the "unmerciful servant". The servant owed the king a large debt. When the king summoned him to pay it, he asked for time to get the money. The king had compassion on him and forgave the entire debt. The servant then went out to collect debts but when his debtors could not pay he became angry and vengeful. The king heard about the servant's ungrateful behavior, summoned him, rebuked him, and had him thrown into jail.

This lesson teaches us the importance of forgiveness in the workplace and the penalty for holding a grudge. Our workplaces may be sources of abundant frustration and pain. We are forced to deal with deceitful coworkers, insensitive bosses, office politics, etc; all of which may fuel feelings of anger and the desire to get revenge. But Jesus teaches us a different standard. We must demonstrate the profound truth of forgiveness not only because God demands it but because our very happiness depends on it. Our words and actions carry tremendous power. We must forgive if we desire forgiveness. Not just once or twice or even seven times. We must forgive every time, every offense, until eternity.

Lord, I don't want my name to be blotted out of the Book of Life. Thank you for helping me to walk in purity, free from unforgiveness, so that I can be listed among your righteous.

NOTES

DAY 11

Work Schedules

The normal work schedule consists of 24 hours per day, 7 days per week, and 365 days per year. The Employer demands a Christ-like image at all times, in public and in private. You are always on duty so overtime is not required.

7In everything set them an example by doing what is good. In your teaching show integrity, seriousness 8and soundness of speech that cannot be condemned, so that those who oppose you may be ashamed because they have nothing bad to say about us. Titus 2:7-8

Christianity is not a religion. It is not what years of misunderstandings have made it. It is not an inaccessible institution obsessed with money, buildings, and self-preservation. It is not church or churchy things. Christianity is not swayed by life's challenges or suppressed by ignorance. And it definitely does not retreat when we clock in at work.

Christianity recognizes that this is God's world and we are accountable to God in everything. Without Him there would be no workplaces, no employers, and no employees; no us. Christianity is a relationship with Jesus that causes our lives to emulate the personal examples, teachings, and values of Jesus. It permeates our existence and helps us to live life as God says it should be not as we know it. Christianity is a lifestyle of limitless possibilities.

Successful workplaces make room for Christ. His spirit is everywhere we are, even in the workplace. It is not confined to churches, ruled by doctrine, or placed on a shelf for special occasions. Christ is not trapped within the pages of our Bible or a name we call on only in times of an emergency.

Many scriptures reveal to us that Christ was always among people where and as they worked. He taught them the importance of their work as service to God. This principle is still applicable today. Our work and everything it encompasses should provide tangible evidence that Christ is in the workplace with us every-day. The words we speak, the work we do, and even the things that go unsaid must all be representative of his presence, his purpose, and his plan. Allowing his example of love, faith, and patience to flourish in us, transforms us. In this transformation, the depth of Christianity is revealed and worship becomes more than a Sunday morning ritual. It becomes a way of life, even at work.

Lord, I want my life to be an example to your people in speech, purity, love, faith, and life. Thank you for setting an example for me to follow and for giving me the desire to follow it.

DAY 12

Promotions

Employees are recruited and selected based on predestined qualifications. These nondiscriminatory methods entitle any qualified person to the rights and privileges of the Employer. It is His intent to promote all individuals who demonstrate the most desirable levels of obedience, faith, and commitment.

5All of you, clothe yourselves with humility toward one another, because," God opposes the proud but gives grace to the humble." 6Humble yourselves, therefore, under God's mighty hand, that he may lift you up in due time. 7Cast all your anxiety on him because he cares for you.1 Peter 5:5-7

Many of us have been passed over for a promotion for which we thought we deserved. Still others have been promoted, transferred, or demoted into situations that were less than desirable. In most instances, our natural response is anger, frustration, or sadness.

Jesus provides us with a roadmap for responding appropriately to the changes in roles, responsibilities, and relationships in the workplace. In 1 Kings 2, Solomon, a 14 year old boy, inherits the throne of his father. King David, Solomon's father, was the most revered leader and had served longer that any previous ruler. This was a tough act to follow but Solomon faced the task at hand with God-lead wisdom.

Three main principles guided his reign. These guidelines remain just a necessary and effective today. Solomon loved the Lord and kept Him first in his life. Unconditional love is the basis of everything we do. Nothing positive or productive can exist without it. Putting God first means thinking of everything we do as an expression of our love for Him. By doing so, Jesus becomes a shield that rebukes the enemy and a magnet that attracts love, joy, peace, and life. Solomon upheld the statutes of his father. As we obey our Heavenly Father, we are strengthened for the task at hand. This strength comes only by developing our relationship with God, keeping his precepts in our daily life, and allowing him to permeate our thoughts and actions. Lastly, Solomon sought out God and worshipped Him often. Throughout our day, we must seek His presence and take time to thank Him even when it seems that there is nothing to be thankful for.

These principles helped Solomon to become just as effective and revered as his father. They will do the same for us. In partnership with Christ, we become positive, patient, and our lives become blessed. With God on our mind and Jesus in our hearts, sin is avoided and we gain victory over our workplace challenges. Even the worst situation becomes a gift and every experience in life becomes an opportunity for promotion.

Lord, transform me into your likeness so that through humility my life becomes a continuous reflection of your glory. Thank you for your grace that removes my anxiety and rewards me with both spiritual and earthly promotion.

NOTES

DAY 13

Rest Periods

The Employer offers unlimited rest periods. No appointment is needed. All requests for rest will be honored. All burden submissions are final.

28"Come to me, all you who are weary and burdened, and I will give you rest. 29Take my yoke upon you and learn from me, for I am gentle and humble in heart, and you will find rest for your souls. Matthew 11:28-29

Cut-backs, lay-offs, and the desire to get as much from one employee as humanly possible have severely damaged the condition of most workplaces and their employees. This greed has resulted in many employees working a 60+ hours week, being on call, and still bringing work home during the weekends. In some companies this has become a common practice that yields great financial gains. But, at what cost?

The cost is damage, death, and destruction. These practices place our mental, physical, and spiritual well-being in jeopardy. They have the potential to compromise the stability of our family, as well. These destructive tendencies isolate us from everything that is important to God like family, peace, and joy. They often leave us feeling incompetent and insecure. They counter our faith. Excessive work hours, preoccupation with work, and the stress associated with just trying to get everything done hinders our ability to operate in the fullness of God. They become deadly distractions that can lead to physical, mental, and spiritual illness.

If Satan can't make us bad, he makes us busy! In our busyness we take our eyes off of God in hopes of seeing our way through the chaos. In the meantime, Satan is having a free-for-all. We find ourselves substituting our time in God's word to read documents from work. Maybe we decide that missing church will provide just enough time for us to complete the report our boss requested. What about the awards banquet for our child that we forgot just because we had a bad day?

While most workaholics would respond by saying, "God knows my heart". There is hope in the Truth. God does know our hearts but even more important is that we know His. We serve an ever-present, strong, creative, and powerful God. He is our relief. His will is that our life at work enhances our being.

Christ desires to be with us, in us, in everything we do. As we welcome Christ into our workplace, we find rest in his strength, creativity, and power. This strength allows us to persevere over the trials of the day. Creativity opens up avenues for navigating over obstacles and utilizing benefits. His power allows us to smile through it all knowing that we are more than conquerors through Him. Keeping Christ in the workplace with us, makes us nurtured instead of annoyed, strengthened instead of shattered, and victorious instead of a victim.

WEARINESS

Lord, as life's burdens try to distract me, I find refuge in you. Thank you for allowing me to come into your presence where I find rest for my weariness and the strength to run the race.

NOTES

____

____

____

____

____

____

DAY 14

Employee At Will

The Employer believes in and adheres to the doctrine of employee-at-will. All employees have the right to terminate their relationship without cause, at any time, for any reason.

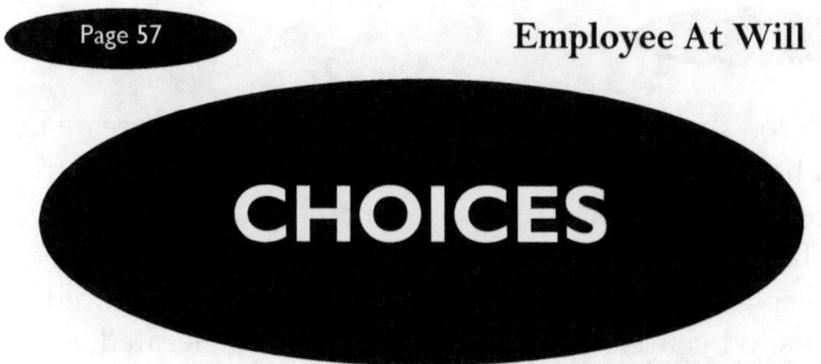

11Let him who does wrong continue to do wrong; let him who is vile continue to be vile; let him who does right continue to do right; and let him who is holy continue to be holy." 12"Behold, I am coming soon! My reward is with me, and I will give to everyone according to what he has done. Revelation 22:11-12

"In God We Trust". But do we? This proclamation, despite its stamp on many things we hold near and dear, has been negated by selfishness and greed. This behavior has not only lead to major corporate scandals but our deterioration as a society, as well. In many companies this belief has been annulled by the "me" syndrome. In an attempt to validate their importance to companies who are only concerned with how much money they can make, many employees have become the center of their own universe. The accumulation of wealth and power has become their primary goal. Anytime a person places themselves before God, we can expect major problems. These sins are destroying individuals and institutions, alike.

The scriptures are filled with stories of people who failed to honor God in the workplace. Their ignorance of God's voice was to their peril. God did not create us to be self-centered gatherers of worldly goods. He created us to be stewards over everything on earth. The Bible is filled with stories of stewards like Abraham, Joseph, Moses, Solomon, and David who experienced the God-centered experience. They all generated, enjoyed, or possessed power and wealth by making God the center of their being. They valued service to others not greed and honor to God not selfishness.

The remedy lies in following the laws already in place to protect people, companies, and assets. These laws are God's laws; to love God, your neighbor, and yourself. We must place God back in his rightful place as the center of our home, our workplace, our country, and our universe. He is the creator of everything and ultimately everything belongs to him. He allows us the privilege of sharing His treasures and provides us the opportunity to share His wealth and prosperity with others. He expects us to respond in thankfulness. As we do the precious cycle starts all over again. As His will becomes our will, there is no lack. All desires to sin are overcome by a passion for Christ and all that He stands for. "In God We Trust" becomes more than a phrase spoken; it becomes a life lived.

Lord, I want to always be in your will therefore I submit myself to you and all your commands for my life. Thank you for giving me clean hands and a pure heart so that I can.

NOTES

____

____

____

____

____

____

BENEFITS & SERVICES

DAY 15

Recognition

Every employee will be rewarded for their conduct, work done, and the cleanness of their hands. Rewards are earned through righteousness. Even those things done in private will be openly rewarded.

HARVEST

11If we have sown spiritual seed among you, is it too much if we reap a material harvest from you? 12If others have this right of support from you, shouldn't we have it all the more? 1 Corinthians 9:11-12

In biblical times, fishing was difficult, dangerous, and often unprofitable. This sounds much like the workplaces of today. Daily we are faced with conflict, confusion, and chaos, especially in the workplace. For many employees, the danger of lying co-workers, conniving bosses, and disloyal employers lies around every corner. But even in this type of workplace lies a blessing.

John 21:3-6 and 10-13 provides a template for harvesting a blessing, even in desperate circumstances. In this story, the disciples had fished all night but caught nothing. Early in the morning, Jesus joins them on the shore and tells them to cast their nets one more time. When they do, they catch so many fish that it was difficult for them to bring in the nets, 153 to be exact. Despite the abundant harvest, the net did not tear. Soon after, Jesus asks them to bring some of the fish and He and the disciples have breakfast together.

So here's the miracle in the message. Jesus longs to join us in the workplace and enrich our lives. In his generosity, he enlarges us and showers us with everything we need to triumph both here on earth and in heaven. In biblical times, these blessings came as healing for the sick, life for the dead, food for the hungry, and provision for those in need. Jesus is still producing the same blessings today in our workplace and in our life

How we respond to His presence dictates the proportion of our harvest. When we selfishly seek out our own desires, we reap pain, disappointment, and failure. But when we freely give a portion of that which he has blessed us with to others, he multiplies that offering. We are flooded with blessings above anything we could ask or imagine. We become valuable, appreciated, and indispensable contributors to our workplace and to the lives of those around us.

Lord, thank you for helping me to faithfully obey the commands that you have given me. I will love you and serve you with all my heart and all my soul. Thank you for sending the rain on my land in its season, so that I can gather a harvest.

DAY 16

Conversions

The Employer reserves the right to make changes to employee plans for the ultimate good. Complete compliance with necessary changes is expected. Successful conversions will be rewarded.

CHANGE

2 "I am about to go the way of all the earth," he said. "So be strong, show yourself a man, 3 and observe what the Lord your God requires: Walk in his ways, and keep his decrees and commands, his laws and requirements, as written in the Law of Moses, so that you may prosper in all you do and wherever you go.1 Kings 2:2-3

Change in the workplace can present opportunities for either grief or growth. Grief often accompanies change associated with a demotion or firing. Yet this same emotion can just as easily accompany a promotion, a lateral move, or simply changes to the company for improvement. Growth on the other hand, is a state of mind. It is recognizing the sovereignty of Jesus, his presence in the workplace, and His power over all circumstances. Growth occurs when we trust Jesus to make all things work for the good of those who love Him and are called according to His purpose. Growth is allowing Christ to transform our mind for the greater good.

Unfortunately, many of us do not have the power to control changes in our workplace. We can, however, control how these changes affect us. Perseverance and endurance through workplace changes comes when we recognize that Christ is always with us, no matter how bad things seem. He is available and willing to intercede on our behalf, every step of the way. Knowing this makes a significant difference in how we respond to change.

Solomon in 1 Kings 2 provides an excellent model for victory through workplace change. He, a 14 year old, was torn away from his life as a pampered prince and thrust into a place of leadership over the nation of Israel. I believe that this presented an enormous task. Not only did he have to deal with grief over the death of his father but now had the responsibility of leading a confused and tempted nation. He was forced to put his own needs aside and to consider the greater needs of the nation entrusted to him.

Solomon's plan for success evolved out of a value system that was not swayed by the waves of change. He humbled himself, declared God to be Lord over him, and worshipped God continuously. For his obedience, God gave him the understanding and discernment he needed to lead. Solomon was a person who wrestled with change, temptation, and failure just as we do. His success came in keeping God as the center of his being. Thorough this commitment, he claimed victory over his workplace obstacles.

We would be wise to follow his example. By doing so, God will give us what we need in life and work to keep the waves of change from crashing against us and causing us harm. He rewards this dedication to Him with the wisdom that we need to lead and to follow. He will not only meet our basic need to cope but will give us the ability to persevere and triumph.

Christ in the workplace transforms our thinking. Changes become stepping stones for opportunity instead of stumbling blocks for grief. Choose Christ, his values and influences, and step right into change as a promotion to the next level of your spiritual walk. Change is inevitable. With Christ, change is growth.

Lord, I know that change is inevitable and that promotion comes only in the presence of change. Thank you for helping me to walk in obedience to you so that I am victorious regardless of the situations I face.

DAY 17

Education

This Employer supplies all employees with wisdom that brings knowledge, understanding, patience, and joy. These attributes are bonafide occupational requirements. A verbal petition to the Employer is required.

17But the wisdom that comes from heaven is first of all pure; then peace-loving, considerate, submissive, full of mercy and good fruit, impartial and sincere. 18Peacemakers who sow in peace raise a harvest of righteousness. James 3:17-18

In the workplace, we are faced with all kinds of darkness. Sadly enough, there is not much we can do to prevent those committed to evil from crossing our paths. What we can do is prepare ourselves to do battle when darkness confronts us. For this, God offers us divine help. He offers us wisdom which serves to comfort us, guide us, and lead us down the right path, His path. Wisdom gives us insight into the God's greater plan for our lives; a plan so much greater than our current circumstances.

Christ is present in our workplace, even in the midst of bad situations. He helps us to cope by giving us Godly insight and direction. He lights our path for clarity. His standard for conduct in the workplace can be seen in James 3:17-18. In this text, James talks frankly about what God expects from us. He explains the importance of honoring Christ's values and how doing so helps us to stay on the course. He explains that wisdom manifests as eight characteristics. Recognizing these characteristics helps us to discern when our actions are less than Godly.

James explains that wisdom is pure, peaceful, considerate, submissive, full of mercy and good fruit, impartial and sincere. Our commitment to these principles manifests as wisdom that rejects human instinct. It rejects the fight or flight response that becomes so innate to us in times of distress. Wisdom reminds us that evil for evil will never overcome evil. Most importantly, it holds the key to conquering evil with Christ's power, his values, and our willingness to take up the cross and follow Him.

We must dedicate every part of our being to God, not just when things are going good but even in the depths of our despair. Godly wisdom provides the energy, purity, and peace to remain calm as evil confronts us. Through our submission to God and love and consideration for others we become full of mercy and our impartial sincerity bears good fruit. This fruit not only tastes good to the kingdom of God, it provides a sweet savor for our employer and our workplace, as well.

Lord, I understand that all the treasures of wisdom and knowledge are hidden in your presence. Thank you that my purpose is to be encouraged in heart and united in love, so that I can have the full riches of complete understanding which keep me on a righteous path.

NOTES

____

____

____

____

____

____

DAY 18

Management

All employees are expected to act in the role of a leader. The employer will provide all necessary tools for success.

4 Then Moses cried out to the Lord, "What am I to do
with these people? They are almost ready to stone me." 5
The Lord answered Moses, "Walk on ahead of the people.
Take with you some of the elders of Israel and take in your hand the staff with which you struck the Nile, and go.
Exodus 17:4-5

In the secular workplace, our value as a leader, is validate by our actions not our beliefs. To the contrary, in the body of Christ, we are justified by our commitment to God, his precepts, and his plan. It does not matter if we clean floors in a small mom and pop business or we are the CEO of a large corporation, we are called to be leaders. But this responsibility is not without challenges. In our quest for success, we may be forced to face anything from frayed nerves and flared tempers to complaining and total defiance.

God offers a timeless and practical leadership manual in Exodus 17. In this text, God uses Moses to reveal the secret to victory in leadership. Moses was chosen by God to lead an enslaved people to freedom. This was at times an overwhelming task. His followers, the Israelites, were distrustful, angry, exhausted, and constantly complaining. In his frustration Moses cried out to God and God honored his openness and honesty with wisdom and guidance. God qualified Moses for every task set before him by giving him three very important leadership tools. These tools remain just as relevant today.

First, Moses was told to go ahead of the people. This prevented him from becoming deterred or discouraged by their negative behavior. Staying in front of the people helped him to maintain his position of authority and not give in to their demands. This reminds me of the concept of being lost in the crowd. God did not want Moses lost in the crowd. He wanted Moses to lead the pack and the only way he could do that was by staying in front and setting the example. When people that we have been chosen to lead complain or resist, we must refuse to become discouraged or hurt by the turmoil. Failure is not an option for the body of Christ. We must cry out to God, listen to His instructions, and continue to press forward.

Second, Moses was told to bring the elders with him. He was to surround himself with wise people who could develop his ideas and test his thoughts. He also needed people around him who would support and encourage him. A lot can be said about the importance of who we as Christians surround ourselves with but the simple fact is that effective leaders are physical signs of God's grace. They are recognized by their level of respect, wisdom, and Godly confidence. We as leaders must surround ourselves with people who can support our commitment to righteousness, encourage us, and correct us when we lose our way.

Last, Moses was to take his staff with him. This symbolized his God-given office and the grace that put him there. It was a reminder that the grace of God was him in his struggles. In the modern day workplace, we don't walk around with a physical staff in our hand. But we should always carry a spiritual staff. This symbol of our God-given authority is apparent when we sow God's word into our hearts, clothe ourselves with righteousness, and live an example for all to follow. When we do, we too lead an enslaved people to freedom and leave our mark in the workplace and on the world.

Lord, I know that I am called to lead but I recognize that I cannot do it without you. Thank you for showing me how use your law as the foundation by which I lead so that I too can guide an enslaved people to freedom though my example.

DAY 19

Health screening

As part of the employment procedure, employees will undergo tests and trials. These trials serve to test the heart and mind as they relate to the Employer's vision. This vision is that each employee walks continuously in the truth, blameless, and with unwavering faith. Every employee will be rewarded according to their conduct and according to what their deeds deserve.

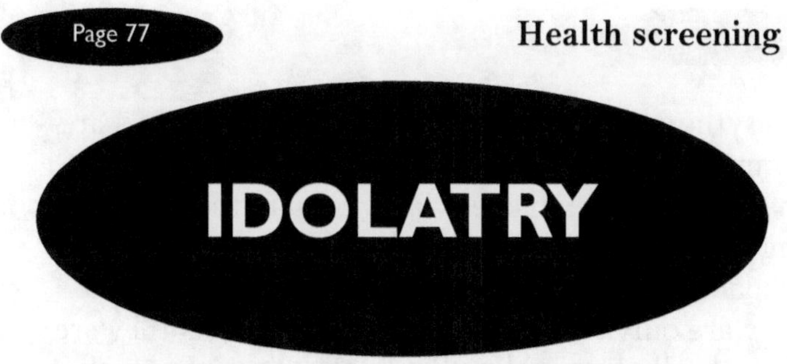

IDOLATRY

15For you did not receive a spirit that makes you a slave again to fear, but you received the Spirit of sonship. And by him we cry, "Abba, Father." 16The Spirit himself testifies with our spirit that we are God's children. 17Now if we are children, then we are heirs—heirs of God and co-heirs with Christ, if indeed we share in his sufferings in order that we may also share in his glory. Romans 8:15-17

The prevailing perception is being a workaholic is an asset. Companies thrive on and reward it. Yet as a workaholic works harder and harder, longer and longer, hoping to gain worth and acceptance; dreams are destroyed, hearts are broken, sickness attacks, and families are destroyed. How many "employees of the year" have traded their family time for dedication to work? How many spouses are forced to carry the entire load of children, work, and home life in the absence of a workaholic spouse? How many church services are missed in the pursuit of perfection in the workplace? Probably more than you could ever imagine.

Recognizing and understanding this as a problem is the first step to overcoming it. Workholism is a disease. It is idolatry. In many cases it places work responsibilities above everything. Often God and everything he values, like family and fellowship, are compromised in the total consumption by work demands. Many employees fall victim to this by allowing their ability or inability to fulfill workplace demands to attack their self-worth. They feel that they are only worthy if their employer feels they are. This deadly lie could not be further from the truth.

Romans 8:14-17 offers us an antidote. In this text, it is revealed to us who we are, whose we are, and our worth because of it. Understanding this scripture helps us to reject the world's ideals about our worth and validation. In verse 15, God is described as "Abba, Father". As we think of God as our father and recognize the idea of a normal father-son or daughter relationship, we gain the understanding that as a child never has to earn a father's love. It is given unconditionally. With Christ in the workplace, we recognize that we do not have to earn our Heavenly Father's love to be worthy. We are worthy because He says we are.

We, as children of God, are joint-heirs to the kingdom with Christ. This not only exposes us to His sufferings but it entitles us to His glory as well. This carries an enormous impact. We are special because we have been chosen by the Heavenly Father. Therefore, we earn the rights and privileges which were given to the Son. Understanding this helps us to strive to be worthy, not because of what we do but because of who we are. This prevents hard work from being confused with the need to be validated by earthly accomplishments.

We should always do our best as we work.

IDOLATRY

Occasionally we may need to put in overtime to complete a task. But we must be careful not to allow our desire to do a good job to be engulfed by the pursuit of worldly accomplishments. By God's grace we are worthy. In this place of righteousness, our work demonstrates that we love what God loves and hate what God hates. This alone represents victory. This success removes the desire to rely on anything other than God. It refocuses our attention on what is really important. Workaholism becomes will, not ours but God's; family becomes first, second only to God; and success transcends what our employer says it is to what God's vision says it is.

Lord, though you probe my heart and examine me; though you test me, you will find nothing contrary to your vision. I have resolved that I will not sin. Thank you for revealing how valuable I am to you. Thank you for being a God that no one or nothing can replace.

DAY 20

Insurance

All employees are guaranteed life insurance through dedication to the purposes of the Employer. This policy provides accidental death and dismemberment. All costs have been paid and the policy never expires. Enrollment is required.

14 For the Lord your God moves about in your camp to protect you and to deliver your enemies to you. Your camp must be holy, so that he will not see among you anything indecent and turn away from you. Deuteronomy 23:14

Many organizations post their goals and vision in public places in hopes that stating them will help others to understand their values. This is exactly what Christians are to do. Jesus gave us a goal and a vision that covers every part of our life, including work. He recorded his instructions in scripture and then validated them by the amazing example of His life and ministry. Through His life he taught the importance of honoring God through our work. Doing so, reveals who we are in Christ and whose values we live by.

Christ wants to share our work experience with us. He wants to share in the fulfillment and meaning of our work as well as the struggles. Having Christ at work does not mean that we will not experience periods of exhaustion or frustration. Even Jesus experienced these feelings. But in His presence, we find protection and strength. With Jesus, we can face whatever life brings us with joy. We can smile in the face of evil and laugh in the presence of pain. Like Jesus, when we grow tired of the battle, we can find refuge in our Heavenly Father. He gives us limitless means to live and work. This improves the quality of our personal and professional lives. It enhances our relationships with the people around us, the work we do, and how we live in general.

Life's setbacks and challenges are an inevitable part of human life but God's generosity will provide everything that we need. He will help us to overcome difficulty in the workplace and in life. He does so with grace. Grace is the manifestation of God's love and undeserved favor. Grace offers us love, peace, strength, joy, protection; whatever we need, when the demands of the secular workplace and the sacredness of God's plan for our life collide. As we abandon our got-it-under-control nature, God's guidance will set us free. This freedom transforms our lives and our workplaces become truly blessed. In this place of blessing, we are protected from the darkness that surrounds us and our light brightens not only our path but the paths of those around us.

Lord, I know that you hear my voice and that you are an ever-present help in the time of need. Thank you for protecting me from the threat of the enemy and those that Satan has chosen to use for his destructive purposes.

NOTES

DAY 21

Voluntary Resignation

Continued failure to comply with job requirements constitutes a voluntary resignation. Employees who voluntarily resign may be afforded the opportunity for re-hire by demonstrating correction of the substandard behavior.

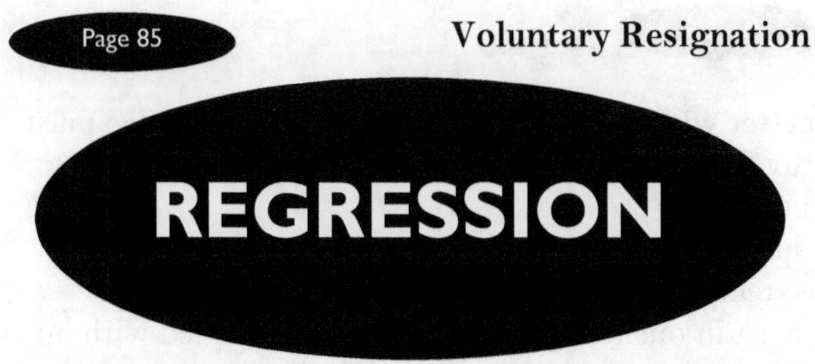

16 Be careful, or you will be enticed to turn away and worship other gods and bow down to them. 17 Then the Lord's anger will burn against you, and he will shut the heavens so that it will not rain and the ground will yield no produce, and you will soon perish from the good land the Lord is giving you. Deuteronomy 11:16-17

Workplaces can place a strain on our relationship with Christ. Sometimes, it is hard to see Jesus when we are forced to deal with angry customers, unrealistic demands, and ungrateful bosses. Not to mention the world's reality that "God stuff" does not belong in the workplace. As much as we would like it to be, the answer is not to cram our Bible down our boss's throat. Surely that would result in some workplace wounds, self-inflicted of course. And I am not suggesting that we start preaching the word of God to everyone we meet. Because trust me, you will become a magnet for more pain.

What I am suggesting is that we not accept the taboo that Christ does not belong in the workplace. No matter where we work or what we face there, we must stay focused on his presence and his precepts. Like a child in the presence of a watchful parent, knowing that Christ is always with us, tempers our actions and our words. Keeping Christ in our thoughts keeps our minds filled with him and not the world around us. Workplace distractions and temptations to sin are avoided. They are replaced by the generosity of Christ and his limitless offers to enjoy life, passion, and aspirations at work.

Success at work demands that we remain faithful to our personal spiritual relationship with Christ. This intimacy should not be limited to our private time but must be maintained publicly through our actions and our words. As evil tries to wrap its cold, rigid grasp around us we can find comfort in the presence of a greater power, a power that guarantees us victory in the face of defeat, joy in the presence of pain, and success in the midst of failure. That power is Jesus.

Lord, I don't want to be a stumbling block to you by participating in sin. Thank you, that through you, Satan is under my feet and I can take up your cross and follow you, even at work.

REGRESSION

DAY 22

Employee Assistance

Each employee is expected to make an eternal effort to overcome their disabilities by repentance and the remission of sins. The Employer will provide supernatural accommodations, unconditional love, and undeserved forgiveness, for those with disabilities. He is committed to your healing and restoration.

STRENGTH

3 Strengthen the feeble hands, steady the knees that give way; 4 say to those with fearful hearts, "Be strong, do not fear; your God will come, he will come with vengeance; with divine retribution he will come to save you." Isaiah 35:3-4

Every day in our workplaces, we are confronted with ideals that are toxic to our spiritual values. It is not uncommon for us to have our confidence diminished by management and co-worker dishonesty or simply the everyday demands of our employer. Still many of us are forced to sit back as our standards are disregarded, our achievements ignored, and positive work relationships damaged. Not to mention, the feelings of pain and anger associated with our institutions simply betraying us.

Often the paths we are forced to take at work are unsafe, confusing, if not deadly. If we choose to walk alone, we become vulnerable to all kinds of darkness and evil. As we try to "handle" the demands of the workplace ourselves, the opposition becomes overwhelming and we often end up feeling helplessness, hopelessness, or just give up. But this is not God's desire for us. His desire is that we overcome these trials with Godly strength and perseverance. But how do we overcome?

There is no magic bullet, quick fix, or formula for victory but there is hope in Jesus. There is a path that we must take. We start by crying out to God and committing ourselves to developing a relationship with him. He comes to our aid with his lamp in hand and provides us with a light that nothing or no one can extinguish. This light gives us clarity and direction. It allows Jesus to take the journey with us and focuses our attention on our spiritual priorities rather than our earthly situations. Perseverance in the struggle requires that we nourish our spiritual growth by remaining committed to both public and private worship and that we constantly build our arsenal of weapons by studying God's word and taking every opportunity to put it to work in our everyday life.

Jesus will navigate the path along the safest and most meaningful path. He stands with us in the face of evil saying, "No need to fear. You will make it". As we stay in Jesus' vivid and revealing light he will guide us through every darkness in our lives and in our workplaces. He will strengthen us for the tasks at hand. His desire is that we be free; free to work and live in peace. Through His strength, we are.

Lord, I want my life to be commendable before you. Therefore, I will endure suffering for doing good and face the trials set before me. Thank you for your example of strength and perseverance in the face of adversity that orders my steps today.

NOTES

____

____

____

____

____

____

DAY 23

Personal Days

Employees are entitled to unlimited personal days. Summoning the Employer requires that you join with other employees who are working toward the eternal vision. In unity the Employer will provide strength and rejuvenation for the tasks at hand. Waste of this precious time is strictly prohibited. Employees who neglect to make arrangements for personal days may be subject to temptation by competing companies.

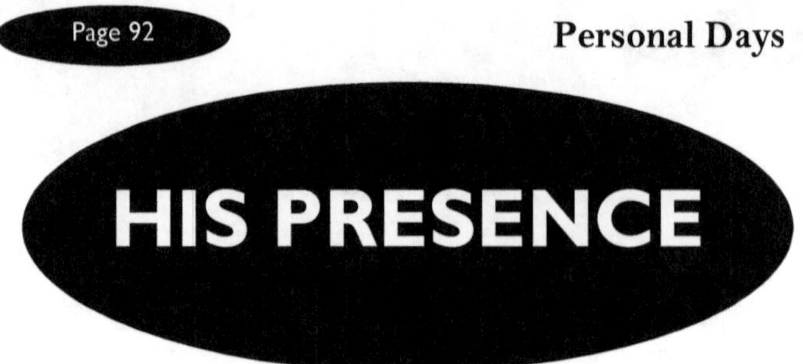

19"Again, I tell you that if two of you on earth agree about anything you ask for, it will be done for you by my Father in heaven. 20For where two or three come together in my name, there am I with them." Matthew 18:19-20

Luke 24:13-36 tells the story of two men who were walking and talking about Jesus. As they discussed Jesus, he came to join them but they did not recognize him. Now keep in mind, these two men were not involved in some deep spiritual act, they were simply "walking and talking" about Jesus. Still Jesus came to walk with them. He began to explain the scriptures concerning himself. The word says that their hearts burned as Jesus opened the scriptures up to them. So you are probably thinking, what does this story have to do with the workplace? Everything!

Most important, this story clarifies the importance of surrounding yourself with God-led people in your workplace. Even in the ungodliness of workplaces, as we surround ourselves with spirit-filled people working toward the things of God, Jesus will be there also. The two men in this story were concerned with the things of God. So much so, that their conversation was devoted to Jesus. And because of it, they were graced with His presence.

Even though they did not recognize him, he still continued to fellowship with them. Even when workplace stress prevents us from feeling Christ's presence, we are not alone. Jesus is with us. Sadly enough, sometimes we too are so caught up in our own situation to recognize. Nevertheless, He will never leave us nor forsake us. This Lord of the world and every workplace is always with us.

Jesus is a companion and resource, like no other. As Jesus joins us in the workplace, he makes his word real to us. This knowledge gives us comfort and encouragement and is vital to helping us to appreciate God and our workplace more fully. Knowledge gives life to our souls. Through it we see past our current circumstances to the strength in our union with other believers. This strength serves to bring a Godly resolution to any circumstance, even at work. It helps us to see our job as it can be with God, not as our employer tries to make it. It provides clarity so that this burden we call a job becomes a blessing that provides for our family and provides the training ground for our spiritual development.

Lord, even though evil surrounds me, I know that I am never alone. Through my union with other believers, your intimate friendship blesses my soul. Thank you for your ever-present Spirit that protects, strengthens, and guides me through life.

NOTES

DAY 24

Sick time

Sick time is strongly discouraged. Employees on sick leave, must submit a verbal resolution and make every effort to return to normal duty. If the employee is unable to return to normal duty with a reasonable period of time, the relationship will be terminated.

ABUSE

1Therefore, since we have been justified through faith, we
have peace with God through our Lord Jesus Christ,
2through whom we have gained access by faith into this
grace in which we now stand. And we rejoice in the hope of
the glory of God. 3Not only so, but we also rejoice in our
sufferings, because we know that suffering produces
perseverance; 4perseverance, character; and character, hope.
5And hope does not disappoint us, because God has poured
out his love into our hearts by the Holy Spirit, whom he has
given us. Romans 5:1-5

No matter where you work or what profession you are in, you will inevitably experience workplace abuse. In today's society, we can expect workplace abuse to be more prevalent than ever. As the lack of self-respect and the lack of respect for others takes dominion over our workplace, so will its accompanying destruction. As long as the predominant ruling lies in worldly values people will continue to hurt other people in the pursuit of success and worldly accomplishments.

Since workplace abuse will probably never go away, we must prepare ourselves to deal with conflict when it comes. Treating our workplace wounds requires that we allow God to lead the way. When we are faced with people who believe that their earthly accomplishments have somehow entitled them to a life of privilege, we must respond in humility, concern, and greatness of spirit. Greatness is not found in titles, achievements, or material wealth. Greatness is the inner quality that flow's from our spirit, the Holy Spirit who lives in us.

As we keep Christ on our minds and in our hearts, the abuse we endure begins to have purpose. That purpose is to build strength and endurance. We grow in our faith which helps us to see that Christ will never abandon us. As we seek His presence, He is there to fight every battle with us. Our union with Jesus brings peace, hope, and love. Within these promises the hurting find hope, the weary find encouragement, the purpose of our pain is revealed, and that which was futile becomes meaningful and valuable.

Lord, though many around me are sick I will not be tempted to sin. I know that you have given me authority over the dark forces that are trying to devour me. Thank you for showing me how to rebuke sin, encourage repentance, and walk in forgiveness.

DAY 25

Funeral Leave

Behavior contrary to the Employer's vision will result in death. Since, the Employer's desire is that all employees have life; each employee will be afforded unlimited opportunities for redemption. A verbal request is required.

4In him was life, and that life was the light of men. 5The
light shines in the darkness, but the darkness has not
understood it. *John 1:4–5*

Living and trying to cope in today's workplaces can blur our vision of Christ. Workplaces that place value on what people do instead of who they are or where process is everything can numb our souls and our perception of our value to Christ. They dampen our discernment of Christ's presence where we work and can accumulate to the point where we become spiritually anesthetized. This leaves us feeling smothered in darkness, unsettled, and alone. In these times we may feel cut of from Christ or wonder if he has abandoned us in the battle.

Sounds a bit dramatic but workplace experiences have such a strong effect on us, since we spend so much of our time there. They not only affect our mind and body but our souls as well. As our souls go neglected for prolonged periods of time, we become a spiritual train wreck waiting to happen.

Most workplaces today have their own particular forms of spiritual darkness from dealing with other people's brokenness to workplace dysfunction. The mission of this darkness is to put out our light. This is Satan's strategic plan for destruction. Unfortunately, we have little power over the presence of these forces. What we do have is the Spirit and light of Christ that keeps Satan's power from gaining control over us.

Jesus promises that he will never abandon us and He doesn't. His light shines even in the midst of the darkest darkness. Nothing can overcome His absolute love and power. Nothing can extinguish His light. Christ's light in us binds the darkness that leaves us broken, exhausted, and drained. It prevents the physical, mental, and spiritual deterioration that Satan so desperately seeks. The light of Christ invigorates and energizes us, leaving us feeling fulfilled and satisfied. Even though darkness will still remain, with the light of Christ guiding us, its power to control and imprison our soul is broken. We are free to live and work in peace, joy, and victory.

Lord, I recognize that you are the gate to life. Through you, I find salvation that keeps the thief from stealing my joy, killing my dreams, and destroying my life. Thank you for coming and lighting my path to righteousness so that I can have life in abundance, even at work.

NOTES

____

____

____

____

____

____

STANDARDS

DAY 26

Conduct

Employees are expected to comply with the rules and regulations of the Employer. This responsibility not only involves walking in sincere respect and love but it also demands that the employee live a life of integrity of heart and uprightness both in public and private.

27Whatever happens, conduct yourselves in a manner worthy of the gospel of Christ. Then, whether I come and see you or only hear about you in my absence, I will know that you stand firm in one spirit, contending as one man for the faith of the gospel 28without being frightened in any way by those who oppose you. This is a sign to them that they will be destroyed, but that you will be saved—and that by God. Philippians 1:27-28

Christianity and dedication to the things of God will not magically change our workplace. As a matter of fact, in the presence of commitment to God, we often find ourselves under constant attack. What maintaining a Christ-like image will do is change the affect that workplace assaults have on us. Keeping Christ with us in the workplace, causes us to shift our priorities from what the world desires to what Christ desires. It focuses our attention on our greater purpose; that of serving God and others with patience, joy, and love. This alone provides a deep sense of peace which guides us through work day tragedies and life in general.

Today's culture of immorality cries out for love. In a

world that glorifies everything evil and dark, we as believers must strive to be the light that overcomes the darkness. Until the world around us sees Christ modeled in our
interactions with one another, they will have a really hard time believing that love exists. One of the most effective ways to reveal the presence of Christ in us is to love one another. For some, our displays of Godly love will be the only tangible love they will ever experience. As we sincerely care for one another, we create an atmosphere where love is contagious. Discord and dissention cannot exist in this environment.

Jesus is not concerned about our resumes or our achievements. He is concerned about our souls. Not only does Jesus tell us to bring our burdens to him, he wants us to "learn from him". No matter how strong we are in Christ, we will struggle with problems in the workplace. It is how we handle those problems that reveal the presence of God in our lives. Learning from Him means maintaining a Christ-like image of unconditional love, humility, and order in everything we do.

Lord, I want people to see the you in me. Thank you for showing me how to conduct my affairs in purity, peace, and love.

DAY 27

Communication

Employees are expected to speak only those things that build up other employees and are in accordance to the vision of the Employer. Foul, negative, or deceitful language is strictly prohibited.

SPEECH

9Do not repay evil with evil or insult with insult, but with blessing, because to this you were called so that you may inherit a blessing. 10For, "Whoever would love life and see good days must keep his tongue from evil and his lips from deceitful speech. 11He must turn from evil and do good; he must seek peace and pursue it. *1 Peter 3:9-11*

In the workplace, hundreds of things will come out of our mouths daily. Choosing to give life with what we say is not always easy. Sometimes things at work become so bad that we wish we could strike someone down with only the words from our mouth. But who wants to compromise eternity for a temporary fix? I surely don't.

Speaking those things that encourage, strengthen, and lovingly correct those around us is essential for productivity and effectiveness. The welfare of our souls and the souls of those around us demand that nothing evil, deceitful, or unwholesome comes out of your mouth. We must limit our speech to words of strength, comfort, and encouragement, even when everything in us wants just the opposite.

God says he will avenge. He is the God of justice. We must walk in obedience knowing that God knows the beginning and end. He knows every intricate detail of our life and is continuously working for our greater good. He will avenge our transgressors.

In the face of workplace trials, avoiding the temptation to complain and gossip means refusing to poison those around us with negativity. It means refusing to compromise our eternal plan. Victory over deceitful, unwholesome, and hurtful speech requires that we stay focused on the positives. It means keeping our mind on Jesus remembering that he is listening to everything we say. Will our speech be a blessing or an insult to the loving compassionate God we serve?

Blessing God with our speech means refusing to allow the negatives in our life to deter and distract us. It means turning these potentially damaging situations into opportunities for growth and spiritual development. Simply said, obedience in speech requires that we look at our life and our workplace through God's eyes. It means accepting our current situation with all of its negatives as temporary training ground and believing for the blessings of God to make all things work for our ultimate good. He will because his word guarantees it. Jesus never lies. He will fulfill all of his promises, in our workplace and in life. (Numbers 23:19)

Lord, I want my words to build others up. I want to speak life into those around me. Thank you for keeping my tongue from evil and allowing my speech to enrich my life and benefit those who listen.

NOTES

DAY 28

Appearance and Dress

Every employee's appearance should reflect that of the Employer. Garment must represent honor, integrity, and strength. Identification badges must be worn at all times. Old patches on new garments are not permitted. Dress-down days are strictly prohibited.

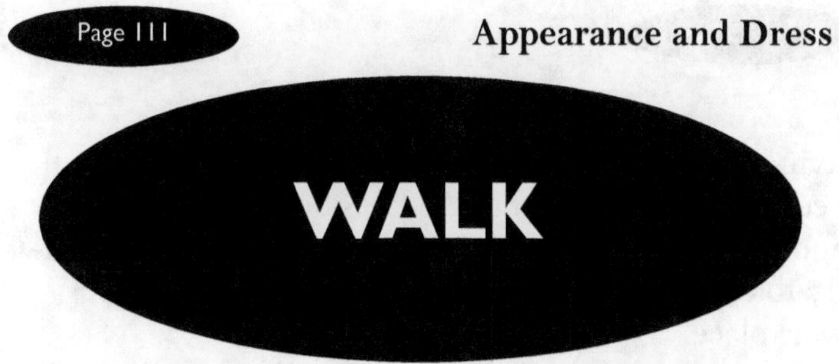

10 I delight greatly in the LORD; my soul rejoices in my God. For he has clothed me with garments of salvation and arrayed me in a robe of righteousness, as a bridegroom adorns his head like a priest, and as a bride adorns herself with her jewels. Isaiah 61:10

The world says that you can't judge a book by its cover. This couldn't be further from the truth. What we, as believers, display for others to see often reflects our inner man. This is especially true in the workplace where we face all types of temptation to fall short, to sin. People who know that we are believers will look for us to set the standard. Those who do not have a relationship with the Lord, desperately need us to be the example.

With the gift of salvation comes the responsibility of being God's messengers. He wants to speak through us. The Devil will tell us that we don't have anything to share but that is a lie. Satan wants to silence our testimony. The truth is that we are a storehouse of experiences, problems, relationships, and temptations that God wants to use to set others free. We are a living testimony to God's sovereignty and love for all people. By sharing what God has done in our lives and the lessons that he has taught us we have the ability to change the world around us, especially in the workplace.

Our testimony lies in our words and our actions. When we, as believers, sin in words or deeds, those who look to us to set the standard become deterred. Who wants to serve a God whose children are angry and distracted? On the other hand, as others see the Christ in us and how his presence transforms us, they will desire to know him. This is an essential part of our purpose here on earth.

God wants us to share our story with others. In some cases, our personal testimony can be much more powerful than any sermon. Our personal experiences and their ability to shape our lives into the image of Christ, will capture the attention of even the most dedicated sinner. Even people who abruptly disapprove of the authority of the Bible will listen to a humbly submitted personal story. They too would be much more willing to mimic behavior that produces positive results such as compassion, love, and patience.

As we walk in obedience to God, good things happen. When others see the blessings over our lives, they will be drawn to the supplier of those blessings. As they seek God, he will make himself real to them and their lives will be forever transformed. This is the fulfillment of our mission in the workplace and in our lives.

Lord, I rend my heart to you today. Thank you for allowing me to enter into your presence where I can he clothed in salvation and righteousness so that I am an blessing to you and those around me.

NOTES

____

____

____

____

____

____

DAY 29

Absenteeism

It is the responsibility of all employees to meet basic standards of intimate time with the Employer. Chronic, habitual, or excessive absenteeism will not be tolerated. This time is necessary for you to meet the demands of service.

*6So then, just as you received Christ Jesus as Lord,
continue to live in him, 7rooted and built up in him,
strengthened in the faith as you were taught, and
overflowing with thankfulness. Colossians 2:6-7*

God has a vision for our lives. It is not temporary or shallow as we see it, it is eternal. It is a desire for us to proper in every aspect of life, even in the workplace. God constantly replays this vision through the working of the Holy Spirit in our lives. His Spirit manifests in the stillness of peace and patience.

The intensely competitive and physically draining workplaces of today are hectic and noisy. In this environment, evil is able to deceive us into complying with the world's way of doing things in hopes of making our workplace challenges more tolerable. Our world has traded peace and quiet for success and worldly promotion even with full knowledge of the power of these behaviors to consume us and deflect our attention from God. This is Satan's way. Satan wants to minimize God's power. He seeks to distract us away from God's ability to guide us through life and strengthen us for the journey.

God is still and quiet. As we learn to face life's challenges with peaceful patience, God is able to make his plans for our life heard. His small voice becomes so clear. In our weakness, God's strength is perfected. We are able to see his plans for us to prosper with clarity. His grace helps us to see life as it can be not as our current circumstances tell us it is.

As workplace trials try to deter and distract us, we must be still and know that He is God. He is present through the fires of life, the storms of workplace drama, and even the stillness of the night. God presence surrounds us. It is personal and intimate. It strengthens us and helps us to endure. It does not come to judge us or to command our lives but to invite us to be still with God. Our ability to persevere over workplace challenges demands that we be open with God, depend on him to guide us, and be willing to allow him to make changes where necessary. In this place of stillness, he offers us the peace, healing, and strength to deal with everyday struggles, at work and in life.

Lord, although you are with me in everything. I know that quiet time with you is required for me to hear your directions for my life. Thank you for welcoming me into your presence where your love and faithfulness helps me to persevere.

NOTES

____

____

____

____

____

____

DAY 30

Theft

Each employee has a predestined job function and purpose within the workplace and is expected to perform within the demands of that job. Acts of theft including coveting, stealing, lust, and jealousy are grounds for disciplinary action.

ENVY

You want something but don't get it. You kill and covet, but you cannot have what you want. You quarrel and fight. You do not have, because you do not ask God. James 4:2

Many workplaces of today encourage a competitive at-any-cost spirit. Occasionally we are put in positions where it seems more effective to step on the backs of our co-workers than to stand up for what is right. Overcoming the desire to covet what others have or to take what does not belong to us in the pursuit of worldly achievements and success requires that we allow God to transform our heart into what he wants it to be; a pure heart.

We are not purified by our own actions or thoughts. Actually, there is nothing that we can do to add to or detract from God's grace. In the midst of the storm, God pours out his grace on our circumstances. His spirit within us produces a pure heart, a heart formed in his image. His reassuring voice speaks into the chaos and darkness around us and calms our fears. This takes our damaged, impure, and fragile heart and turns it into a heart that is whole, pure, and purposeful.

We are transformed completely by the power of God. His living water flowing through us purifies us from all sin. We gain the faith to believe that God has a plan and purpose for our life. He has a path that we will take and ultimately all things will work out for the greater good. This translates to the completeness of God's provision.

Our job is to submit. Victory in this area of life demands that we confess any sin and acknowledge the need for Christ in our lives. We must focus our heart on the things that matter most to God and avoid letting anything hinder our ability to align our lives with his word. This includes the desire to take what doesn't belong to us whether it is another person's spouse or a paperclip. Sin is sin to God. As we align our words and actions with God's word, our fleshly, cynical, and covetous heart begins to believe that God will provide all of our needs according to his glorious riches. Our desire to obey renews our heart and through that renewal we get a fresh start; a new start for righteousness; a new start for life.

Lord, the enemy is tempting me to desire things that are not mine to have. But I recognize these thoughts as sin. I rebuke his attempts right now. Thank your for giving me the faith to believe that you will meet all of my needs.

ENVY

DAY 31

Soliciting

Employees are expected to solicit new employees for the Employer's glory. Acceptable methods include verbal, written, and living models. Living models are preferred in the workplace as many facilities prohibit open promotion of the Employers vision.

39Many of the Samaritans from that town believed in him because of the woman's testimony, "He told me everything I ever did." 40So when the Samaritans came to him, they urged him to stay with them, and he stayed two days. 41And because of his words many more became believers. John 4:39-41

A workplace is wherever we perform a service for someone else. It does not matter if that workplace is a big corporation, a school, or your home. A workplace could even be somewhere where you volunteer your time. In most workplaces, secular culture has tried to separate us from our faith. Unfortunately, we gain value in the workplace not by who we are as a person but by what or how much we can produce.

While these secular values dominate many workplaces, as believers, this cannot be our reality. Our reality testifies to the presence of Christ in our workplace. It places emphasis on our impact in the spirit realm rather than our accomplishments in the earth realm

Since, many workplaces strongly prohibit any display of spirituality. Being a living, breathing, model of

Christ provides the best chance of others coming to know Jesus.

The woman at the well is an excellent representation of
the impact of God's presence on us, our co-workers, and our workplace as a whole. In John 4:5-42, Jesus, while in Samaria, met a woman a well. She had come from her workplace in the home to get water from the well. As Jesus asked her for a drink she questioned his right to speak to her since he was a Jew and she was a Samaritan. The prejudice between the two cultures was deep-seated. Nevertheless, Jesus made himself real to her. He validated her worth as a person and as someone who could be loved by God. His ministry and her willingness to receive it radically changed her life.

In our workplaces, it is highly likely that we will meet someone who will transform us or be transformed by our actions. By expecting our workplace to be as God wants it to be instead of the way we know it, we are able to perform with assurance in God's presence, his sovereignty, and his willingness to love and guide us. People love to give and receive good news. As we demonstrate God's presence in our words and our actions, we share the good news about Jesus with others. By doing so, they come to know Jesus and their lives, like the Samaritan woman, will be dramatically and eternally changed.

Lord, I know that my workplace calls for creativity in the area of witnessing. Thank you helping me to be an example of your presence in the workplace. Thank you for helping to live a good life, one that glorifies you and reveals your glory to those around me.

NOTES

____

____

____

____

____

____

DAY *32*

Blood Exposure

Employees are expected to be exposed to the Blood at all times. Protective armor is necessary to prevent blood leaks. If a leak occurs, it must immediately be cleaned up and the opening closed through militant prayer and obedience.

10 Moses said to the Lord, "O Lord, I have never been eloquent, neither in the past nor since you have spoken to your servant. I am slow of speech and tongue." 11 The Lord said to him, "Who gave man his mouth? Who makes him deaf or mute? Who gives him sight or makes him blind? Is it not I, the Lord? 12 Now go; I will help you speak and will teach you what to say." Exodus 4:10-12

In the workplace, many of us are shackled by our belief that we are what the world says we are. We learn this misconception either by our own negative experiences in the workplace or it is planted by others whose negativity has influenced us. Envious co-workers, incompetent bosses, or arrogant customers all contribute to the toxic ground that demeans our abilities and worth as human beings. Even more damaging is allowing our own accomplishments to validate our greatness. This "can-do-it-by-myself" attitude is an accident waiting to happen.

How we perceive ourselves will either limit or enrich our ability to see our greatness. There is greatness in all of us, not because of anything we have done. Our greatness is also not affected by anything we can do, either. It is a gift from God. It is how God made us. He wants us to live in its fullness. We are uniquely made by God. He carefully selected every aspect of our being. He designed us for greatness and his plan will ultimately be fulfilled in all of us.

Look at Moses in the text above. He felt less than equipped to lead because of his speech impediment. He felt that someone, anyone would be better. But God's greatness in him was not hindered by his lack of faith. God was persistent. He was committed to Moses' fulfillment of his purpose. Because of this, Moses became one of history's greatest leaders.

This same greatness is wonderfully distilled in us; all of us. With God, we too can do remarkable things. We are made in the image of God who is great. Therefore we are great. We must focus on his clear and present plan for our lives and ask him to give us the wisdom and strength to live it out. As we go with God, we learn to soar in the workplace and in life. We learn to let the greatness of God, work through and in us. By doing so, we become effective in every work, beyond anything we could ever ask.

Lord, I don't ever want your blood to leak from me through sin. I want it to be ever secure. Thank you for showing me how to walk upright so that your blood is secure and the grace and peace it brings purifies and sanctifies me. Thank you for helping me to see your greatness in me.

NOTES

____

____

____

____

____

____

DAY 33

Grievance

The Employer is committed to justice and resolving all employee issues in a timely manner. All appeals are handled in a confidential and timely fashion.

11"Blessed are you when people insult you, persecute you and falsely say all kinds of evil against you because of me. 12Rejoice and be glad, because great is your reward in heaven, for in the same way they persecuted the prophets who were before you. Matthew 5:11-12

For poorly treated employees, the pain may be awful. The healing process may be even worse. It is as if the crucifixion nails are being hammered into our hands and feet for something we didn't do. Sounds familiar?

Workplace mistreatment and the resulting wounds damage the well-being of employees, their families, and the organization. Abuse and neglect in the workplace causes employees to question the fruitfulness of their actions. Those wounded by ill-treatment usually end up feeling doubtful, insecure, and hurt. These sins are detrimental to the fulfillment of our purpose. Even the most committed Christians, may question God's presence in the midst of such a breech of trust and loyalty. Healing from this betrayal demands that we stand on our Christian ethics, grounded in the values of Jesus.

Only these are absolute.

Jesus is Lord of the workplace and all creation. He is Lord over us. In the face of this evil, remember to whom we are responsible and for what. We must focus on loving people and loving ourselves. Loving people means walking in forgiveness and joy even in the midst of the pain. Loving ourselves requires that we remember that we are created in the likeness of God to rule over the earth. We have eternal value. No earthly being or situation can change that. We must believe that we are what God says we are, not as the world or our employer views us. Even though the world's value of us may lessen, God's view of us never changes. He loves us and desires for us to have abundant life, not just at home or in church but in the workplace as well.

Mistreatment in the workplace is a violation of God's laws. We may not have power over the one who mistreated us but we do have power over how we deal with their sin. We have two choices. We can scamper away in defeat or we can stand on God's truths? I believe that the closing of one door means that God has another more profitable door open and waiting for us. The only battle that the devil ever wins is the one we don't fight. Fight for righteousness. Claim your victory, your healing, and step right into that open door of opportunity.

I, your chosen one, is crying out for honesty and integrity. Thank you for being the God of justice. Thank you for hearing my cries and for making the unjust just.

NOTES

____

____

____

____

____

____

DAY 34

Fire Safety

This Employer provides a smoke-free environment. Those who choose to smoke will be confined to the only designated smoking area, Hell. Smoking cessation programs will be offered throughout your employment free of charge.

*8If your hand or your foot causes you to sin, cut it off and
throw it away. It is better for you to enter life maimed or
crippled than to have two hands or two feet and be thrown
into eternal fire. 9And if your eye causes you to sin, gouge it
out and throw it away. It is better for you to enter life with
one eye than to have two eyes and be thrown into the fire of
hell. Matthew 18:8-9*

In today's culture, we are confronted with sin on a daily basis. The workplace is no exception. As a matter of fact, many companies today are breeding grounds for all kinds of darkness. These environments thrust us into situations that tempt us to respond in hatred, revenge, anger, and everything else contrary to God's word.

How we respond will inevitably bring a smile or a frown to God's face. To help us respond in a manner that brings joy to God, he gave us the Holy Spirit who comes to live in us and work through us. His Spirit is available to anyone who asks and receives. Through the presence of this creatively working Spirit we are enabled in every way imaginable. We are blessed with courage, supernatural abilities, patience, and wisdom. We are compelled to generously pour our God's love on those around us.

The Holy Spirit living in us is evidenced by our willingness to live and work in love, peace, and joy. As we face darkness in the workplace and in life, we must strive to help each person to know God's love. This can only be done when we respond to life's challenges as Christ would; with God's word and his example of humility and compassion.

Occasionally the workplace tries to grind it into us that we are ordinary people. And yes we are. But we are also extraordinary people moved by an extraordinary God to do extraordinary things. Our willingness to obey his commands and to allow his Spirit to form our response to sin, multiplies our value exponentially. Our lives are different because of it. More importantly, we are able to reproduce the life of Christ in others.

This serves to gently remind us that God is with us, now and forever; in our hearts, in our homes, and in our workplaces.

Lord, I know that sin corrupts my temple. I want to build it up by avoiding anything that corrupts me. Thank you for teaching me how to cut off the parts of my body and my life that seek to condemn me to hell's fire.

NOTES

____

____

____

____

____

____

DAY 35

Worker's Compensation

Work-related accidents, without regard to magnitude, must be reported immediately to the Employer. Witnesses to workplace injury are expected to seek immediate Employer assistance on behalf of the injured employee. All treatment is provided free of charge.

.

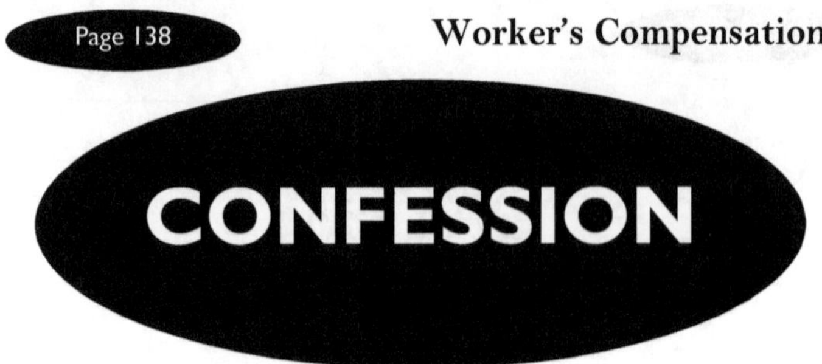

12 When the righteous triumph, there is great elation; but when the wicked rise to power, men go into hiding. 13 He who conceals his sins does not prosper, but whoever confesses and renounces them finds mercy. Proverbs 28:12-13

Do you ever feel like your behavior has been so bad that God could never make it right? Sounds dumb when we say it out loud but I think at some point, especially in the midst of life's storms, we all think it. Many of us fear that our sins will cause God to no longer love us or that we have gone beyond the reach of his patience and grace. The truth is that nothing we could do would ever make God stop loving us. There is no sin that he can't redeem and no mistake that he won't make right. When the enemy brings these feelings of fear and abandonment to us, we must run full-throttle into God's grace. His grace which is rooted in prefect love comforts our fears.

We can approach God's throne of grace boldly. He is always willing to accept us and love us back to righteousness. His grace is so infinite and powerful that it murders grief,
guilt, and sin. It transforms our life into a life that represents his holy plan and purpose. That plan is built on the foundation of his unconditional love for us. This love brings redemption, restoration, and deliverance.

Receiving his grace requires our humble and sincere confession and our desire to work towards a return to righteousness. As we confess our sins, God breathes his holiness into us. It saturates every fiber of our being. By this, we are transformed into what God says we are, righteous and holy. We find strength in the reassurance that God's grace is greater than any of our sins. His love is deeper than our fears. And his presence is stronger than our faults, our mistakes, and our failures.

I know that confession helps me to walk in freedom. Therefore I confess my sin/s of ______________________ right now. Thank you for your undeserved forgiveness which helps me to break free from the sin that binds me.

DAY 36

Sleeping on Duty

Sleeping is not permitted while on duty. Doing so will allow the competition to manipulate you into behavior that is contrary to the vision of the Employer. Employees found violating this policy will be subject to unnecessary setbacks and avoidable obstacles.

35"Therefore keep watch because you do not know when the owner of the house will come back—whether in the evening, or at midnight, or when the rooster crows, or at dawn, 36 If he comes suddenly, do not let him find you sleeping. 37What I say to you, 1 say to everyone: 'Watch!' Mark 13:35-36

We are called to fulfill God purpose in every aspect of life. This plan includes worship, fellowship, growth, and service. God does not want some of us part of the time. God needs all of us, all of the time, to fulfill his plan.

Satan seeks to hinder our fulfillment of this plan through distraction. He places things in our path that take our eyes off of God. He knows our weaknesses and he not afraid to use them. This is why it is so important that we as believers remain diligent in the things of God and vigilant against the attack of the enemy.

Diligence means refusing to sin. When we do sin,

diligence means acknowledging and confessing that sin and trusting God to redeem and restore us. It means doing our part to live lives of spiritual significance.

Vigilance is knowing that the devil is real. It is sowing enough of God's word into our lives and into our hearts that we can see Satan from a mile away. We are able to see his destructive plan and to recognize circumstances being created for the fulfillment of that deadly plan. It is always being prepared to do battle; not just for ourselves but for others as well. Vigilance means having clean hands and a pure heart so that our prayers for protection, strength, and victory are not hindered by sin.

In the workplace we will face all kinds of darkness. Occasionally Satan will trick us into stepping off the path. Vigilance is knowing that we serve a Heavenly Father who loves us unconditionally. He is always ready and willing to supply all of our needs. He longs to shower us with grace which gives clarity to the confused, vision to the lost, restoration to the wounded, and redemption the sinner. Vigilance is trusting God to be everything we need, in every environment, in every situation.

Lord, I don't want to be caught off guard by sin. When you knock, I want to be able to immediately open the door for you. Thank you for your faithfulness that strengthens me and protects me from the evil one so that I am always dressed and ready for service.

NOTES

____

____

____

____

____

____

DAY 37

Performance Review

Employees will be subject to continuous examination by the Employer. This appraisal is intended to measure effectiveness. Employees will be notified immediately of any areas of weakness and is expected to make the necessary adjustments to bring his or her performance into compliance.

SERVICE

16By their fruit you will recognize them. Do people pick grapes from thorn bushes, or figs from thistles? 17Likewise every good tree bears good fruit, but a bad tree bears bad fruit. Matthew 7:16-17

In a society where workplaces are becoming more uncivil, antagonistic, and temperamental; God offers us many templates for dealing with other people's behavior in a constructive way. One example is Luke 12. God uses this text to teach us an important lesson about control in the face of temptation to sin. Luke 12:13-21 tells the story of two brothers who are arguing over an inheritance. They ask Jesus to arbitrate. Instead he teaches them a lesson about applying themselves. This lesson is still applicable today.

The first thing Jesus did was listen. Sometimes listening is all we need to do to resolve a conflict. When we actively listen to what is being said to us, we are able to get the full understanding of the issue. Listening also portrays concern for the opponent's plight. This at times is all the other person needs to feel understood. This often makes for a quick resolution.

Second, Jesus did not engage in the conversation. He refused to take sides. Instead he offered an impartial word of

correction. Remaining impartial when drawn into a disagreement between others prevents us from becoming the scapegoat for anger and frustration. It affords us the opportunity to offer words of correction and clarity to the situation. We may even be able to end the controversy by not adding fuel to the fire.

Last, Jesus gave the two brothers a higher principle. He was able to recognize the catalyst of their argument as greed and he was able to redirect their actions. When we are drawn into conflict either as a participant or a witness, we must be willing to take the high road. We must be willing to step down in humility knowing that ultimately, God is the judge and jury. He will make every situation right and we must trust him to do so.

Avoiding or ending conflict in the workplace requires that we stay focused on what really matters. Our priorities must be what matters most to God. Even though he desires that we live and walk in his image, God gives us the right to choose. We can choose to respond by being uncivil and angry or we can make the choice to align our reactions with God's word. Although door number one may offer immediate gratification, door number two has eternal value. It offers victory over the things that bind us and freedom from workplace conflict.

Lord, I want my life to show others the You in me. Thank you for your word and your example which teaches me how to bear good fruit.

NOTES

____

____

____

____

____

____

DAY 38

Disciplinary Actions

Any employee who violates the rules of the Employer is subject to disciplinary action. This disciplinary action may take the form of private or open rebuke, suspension, or discharge. Immediate remediation of the substandard behavior is necessary for restoration to your current employment status.

Procedure for Disciplinary Actions:

1. Holy Spirit conviction is the most important facet of this program.
2. All sin is considered equal.
3. All warnings should be immediately heeded.
4. No employee will be unduly penalized as the Employer is a God of justice.

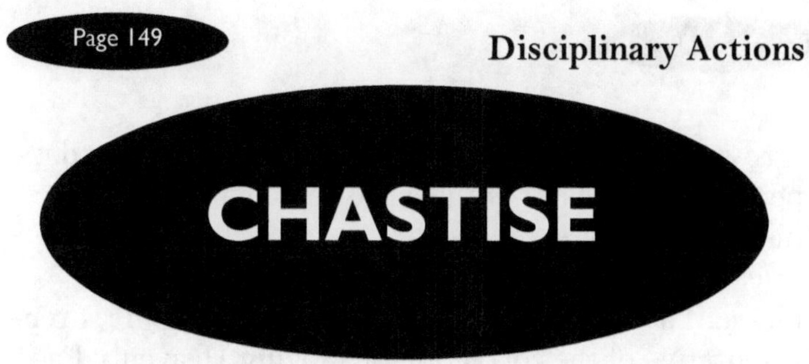

CHASTISE

11 My son, do not despise the Lord's discipline and do not resent his rebuke, 12 because the LORD disciplines those he loves, as a father the son he delights in. Proverbs 3:11-12

Few Christians understand what it means to be chastised by the Lord. Many have never even heard his voice. In my 17 years as a member of a denominational church the concept of chastisement was never even mentioned much less explained. But it is something that every Christian should learn about. The success of our Christian walk depends on it.

Hebrews 12:11 describes discipline as unpleasant and painful. But even more important is the explanation of the purpose of chastisement. The scripture says that it produces a harvest of righteousness and peace. It is not meant to destroy us but to lead us to repentance. Psalm 94:12 tells us that it teaches us God's law. This is why being able to hear God's voice and his instruction for our life is so vital. God wants what is best for us. He wants us to have life, not death. For this reason, he will discipline us if we persist in sin or have grown indifferent to his plans for our lives. Jesus desperately desires our enthusiasm and commitment to his eternal plan.

Jesus' rebuke is motivated by love. Although unpleasant at times, it is never a negative thing. It is representative of the correction of a loving Heavenly Father toward his children. As a Father to some occasionally unruly children, God finds the need to correct us with a spiritual spanking when our sin and rebellion makes is necessary. Think back to when we were children. Occasionally we did something that required the discipline of our parents. Even when the spanking hurt, we knew that our parents loved us. As we grew older and more mature, we were able to see the importance of their correction to our growth and success.

Spiritual chastisement is personal. I believe that it based on our spiritual maturity. When I rededicated my life back to the Lord, he took it easy on me. When the Holy Spirit spoke to me I recognized the need to make changes to my life but his voice of correction was a calm and reassuring voice. As I grew spiritually, so did his demands for my obedience. His voice became firm, clear, and precise. His voice drew immediate results from me and it still does to this day.

Not all of our troubles are the result of spiritual chastisement. Some of them are the result of the attack of the enemy. John 10:27 says, "My sheep listen to my voice; I know them, and they follow me." If we are truly Jesus' sheep, then we must learn to recognize our Heavenly Father's voice and to hear with clarity his instructions for our life. As we respond to his rebuke in humility and repentance, he restores us. In this restoration, we not only find healing, growth, and prosperity; we find the compassionate arms of a persistent Father waiting to love us and propel us into a place of righteousness and purpose.

Lord, I welcome your rebuke for the things that I have done that are contrary to your word. Thank you for loving me enough to discipline me so that my life can be one that you delight in.

DAY 40

Retirement

The Employer offers an enhanced retirement plan. Employees contribute by upholding the vision of the Employer at all times. All eligible employees are entitled to an Employer contribution greater than their own.

ETERNITY

10God is not unjust; he will not forget your work and the love you have shown him as you have helped his people and continue to help them. 11We want each of you to show this same diligence to the very end, in order to make your hope sure. 12We do not want you to become lazy, but to imitate those who through faith and patience inherit what has been promised. Hebrews 6:10-12

Enjoying eternity requires our obedience here on earth. It is not limited to just our service in church but everything we do that glorifies the Lord, even our work in the workplace. These practices sometimes so contradict the way of the world that we find ourselves under attack. This attack as described in scripture is an invisible force. This invisible force, Satan, uses many people, situations, and circumstances to challenge our commitment to the things of God.

As a result of our culture's disdain for biblical obedience, an increasing number of Christians find ways around God's rules to make themselves and their lives comfortable. This is a deadly mistake. We must avoid maneuvering around God's word for the sake of human or cultural bias. We must claim his rules and instructions as our law and not settle for anything less. Even when modern culture seems to outweigh our need to obey God's word, we must allow His everflowing grace and Holy Spirit conviction to lead the way.

With Jesus in our lives and in our workplace, there is never confusion about obedience. God's word is clear and specific for every aspect of life. Through obedience we work out our faith in practice. If we truly believe God's word, then we obey without hesitance. We walk in genuine faith which helps us shun whatever might offend God or discredit his name. Paul explains penalties for those who refused to obey. He tells the church that they should no longer fellowship with people who were disobedient or they would miss the familiar loving warmth of the fellowship and "be ashamed" of their failure to follow God's Law. Those who do not run the race or do not compete according to the rules will not receive the victor's crown.

God takes obedience seriously. Obedient living in submission to Christ will bring about an eternal reward when Christ returns. Obedience "without spot or blame", brings a glorious outcome. Those who run the race will receive a crown of blessedness as an eternal reward from Jesus Christ. Are you running the race? Following the rules? Jesus is coming back and his reward is with him. He will reward everyone according to what he or she has done for and in the kingdom. Our obedience given freely, in genuine love, compassion, humility, and faith helps us to claim this reward. Living in joyful, humble obedience promises a wonderful reward when we are called to our heavenly home to join Christ for eternity.

Lord, I want to live and not die,
Therefore I have committed my life to doing what is just and right. Thank you for helping me to turn from wickedness so that I can have eternal life.

DAY 41

Reward

Employees are rewarded for excellence in service. Each employee will be compensated according to the measure of that which has been sown.

8The one who sows to please his sinful nature, from that nature will reap destruction; the one who sows to please the Spirit, from the Spirit will reap eternal life. 9Let us not become weary in doing good, for at the proper time we will reap a harvest if we do not give up. 10Therefore, as we have opportunity, let us do good to all people, especially to those who belong to the family of believers. Galatians 6:8-10

Success demands that we distinguish between power and responsibility. Power is what the world tells us is important. Power is control that we gain through our own actions and appointments. It is control of things that are not ours to control. It is self-appointed and self-endorsed. When we take God out of any aspect of our lives, corruption and immorality prevails. Responsibility is what is important to God and eternity. It is intensely personal. It signifies true success.

Responsibility is the basis for Christian stewardship. Stewardship does not just cover the aspect of managing money. It includes being a shepherd over every thing that God has blessed us with including our family, our friends, our homes, and our workplaces.

Stewardship is a way of life that validates that everything in our life belongs to God.
Because it belongs to God, it is a blessing to be cherished and nurtured.

Stewardship calls us to be leaders in our Christian life and anywhere else we are. It is evangelism. It is making a choice to honor God in our attitude, our actions, and our material possessions. Through our obedience we reveal our relationship with Christ to those around us. Our humble confidence serves as a visible sign of how precious Christ is to us. This tells others, even our boss, who's really the boss, Jesus Christ.

We cannot serve two masters. We must choose whom we will love. Do we love money and success so much so that we are willing to compromise our Godly commitment? Or do we love the Lord so deeply that we see everything in our life as a blessing from Him and we desire to keep watch over how every aspect of our life is managed? When we choose the latter then we have chosen stewardship and its many rewards. Choosing stewardship means that we are storing up treasures in Heaven, were moths and rust cannot corrupt. We are converting our work here on earth into heavenly currency. Stewardship makes us truly wealthy and this wealth no man can take away.

Lord, although I understand that heavenly treasure is most important, money is necessary for my existence here on earth. Thank you for providing this earthly job which is just one of the many ways that you meet my needs. Thank you for providing opportunities for me to sow spiritual seeds so that I can reap a harvest.

NOTES

SHAREHOLDER AGREEMENT

The Body of Christ
PLEDGE TO EXCELLENCE IN SERVICE

I understand that the body of Christ is committed to being the best of the best in the provision of Godly service and strives to honor God in everything. It desires to have people on its team who care about people and long to help others. I also understand that the promotion of this body depends 100% on the commitment of each individual to the cooperative efforts. Therefore, I agree to accept a partnership with this body in its commitment to excellence in service, I will S.T.E.P. up to the challenge through the following:

SERVICE
I agree to serve others by using my gifts, faithfully to administer God's grace to those around me.

TESTIFY
I agree to promote the gospel in my work by setting an example of responsibility, honesty, accountability, and strength through Jesus Christ.

EDIFY
I agree to build up God's people by remaining positive, peaceful, respectful, and caring at all times.

PERSEVERE
I agree to honor God with faithfulness in my work and by remaining Christ-like under any circumstance.

Sometimes the challenges of my daily duties may cause me to question this pledge. But greater is He who is in me than he who is in the world. I will remember always the sacrifice of Jesus and how difficult it must have been for an innocent man to die for the guilty; to die for ME. Then I will extend myself to Him so that he will give me the strength to provide a service that far exceeds worldly expectations.

____

Signature:

www.ingramcontent.com/pod-product-compliance
Lightning Source LLC
LaVergne TN
LVHW021455080426
835509LV00018B/2292

* 9 7 8 0 9 7 8 8 5 4 5 5 3 *